100 BEST

4 Ingredient

RECIPES

Publications International, Ltd.

Favorite Brand Name Recipes at www.fbnr.com

Copyright © 2003 Publications International, Ltd.
All rights reserved. This publication may not be reproduced or quoted in whole or in part by any means whatsoever without written permission from:

Louis Weber, CEO
Publications International, Ltd.
7373 North Cicero Avenue
Lincolnwood, IL 60712

Permission is never granted for commercial purposes.

Favorite Brand Name is a trademark of Publications International, Ltd.

All recipes and photographs that contain specific brand names are copyrighted by those companies and/or associations, unless otherwise specified. All photographs *except* those on pages 105, 109 and 119 copyright © Publications International, Ltd.

Some of the products listed in this publication may be in limited distribution.

Pictured on the front cover: Marinated Pork Roast *(page 80)*.
Pictured on the back cover *(clockwise from top left):* Mexican Roll-Ups *(page 10)*, Hidden Valley® Broiled Fish *(page 88)*, Chocolate Mint Ravioli Cookies *(page 114)* and Oven-Roasted Vegetables *(page 34)*.

ISBN-13: 978-1-4127-9661-3
ISBN-10: 1-4127-9661-X

Manufactured in China.

8 7 6 5 4 3 2 1

Microwave Cooking: Microwave ovens vary in wattage. Use the cooking times as guidelines and check for doneness before adding more time.

Preparation/Cooking Times: Preparation times are based on the approximate amount of time required to assemble the recipe before cooking, baking, chilling or serving. These times include preparation steps such as measuring, chopping and mixing. The fact that some preparations and cooking can be done simultaneously is taken into account. Preparation of optional ingredients and serving suggestions is not included.

Contents

Alluring
APPETIZERS

Bacon-Wrapped Breadsticks

8 slices bacon
16 garlic-flavored breadsticks (about 8 inches long)
¾ cup grated Parmesan cheese
2 tablespoons chopped fresh parsley (optional)

1. Cut bacon slices in half lengthwise. Wrap half slice of bacon diagonally around each breadstick. Combine Parmesan cheese and parsley, if desired, in shallow dish; set aside.

2. Place 4 breadsticks on double layer of paper towels in microwave oven. Microwave on HIGH 2 to 3 minutes or until bacon is cooked through. Immediately roll breadsticks in Parmesan mixture to coat. Repeat with remaining breadsticks.   *Makes 16 breadsticks*

Arizona Cheese Crisp

Vegetable oil for deep-frying
2 (10- or 12-inch) flour tortillas
1 to 1½ cups (4 to 6 ounces) shredded Cheddar or
   Monterey Jack cheese
½ cup picante sauce
¼ cup grated Parmesan cheese

1. Pour oil into wok to depth of 1 inch. Place over medium-high heat until oil registers 360°F on deep-frying thermometer. Slide 1 tortilla into oil. Using 2 slotted spoons, gently hold center of tortilla down so oil flows over edges. When tortilla is crisp and golden on bottom, carefully tilt wok, holding tortilla in place with spoon, to cover edge of tortilla with oil; cook until lightly browned. Rotate tortilla as needed so entire edge is lightly browned. Remove from oil and drain on paper towels, curled side down. Repeat with second tortilla. Tortillas can be made up to 8 hours in advance. Cover loosely and let stand at room temperature.

2. Preheat oven to 350°F. Place shells, curled side up, on baking sheet. Sprinkle each with half of Cheddar cheese; top each with half of picante sauce. Sprinkle with Parmesan cheese. Bake, uncovered, 8 to 10 minutes or until cheeses melt. To serve, break into bite-size pieces.

Makes 4 to 6 servings

Chorizo Cheese Crisp: Remove casing from ¼ pound chorizo sausage. Crumble sausage into large skillet; stir over medium-high heat until browned. Drain fat. Follow directions for Arizona Cheese Crisp but substitute chorizo for Parmesan cheese.

Olive Cheese Crisp: Follow directions for Arizona Cheese Crisp but omit picante sauce and Parmesan cheese. Sprinkle ⅓ cup sliced pitted ripe olives and ⅓ cup diced green chiles over Cheddar cheese.

Can't Get Enough Chicken Wings

18 chicken wings (about 3 pounds)
 1 envelope LIPTON® RECIPE SECRETS® Savory Herb with Garlic
    Soup Mix
 ½ cup water
 2 to 3 tablespoons hot pepper sauce* (optional)
 2 tablespoons margarine or butter

Use more or less hot pepper sauce as desired.

1. Cut tips off chicken wings (save tips for soup). Cut chicken wings in half at joint. Deep fry, bake or broil until golden brown and crunchy.

2. Meanwhile, in small saucepan, combine soup mix, water and hot pepper sauce. Cook over low heat, stirring occasionally, 2 minutes or until thickened. Remove from heat and stir in margarine.

3. In large bowl, toss cooked chicken wings with hot soup mixture until evenly coated. Serve, if desired, over greens with cut-up celery.
Makes 36 appetizers

quick tip

The tips from the chicken wings can be used to make your own chicken stock. Simmer wing tips with water, onion, celery, bay leaf and any other vegetables or herbs you desire for 1 to 2 hours. Strain stock and skim off the fat. Freeze in containers or self-closing plastic bags for later use.

Alluring Appetizers

Zesty Bruschetta

1 envelope LIPTON® RECIPE SECRETS® Savory Herb with Garlic
    Soup Mix
6 tablespoons olive or vegetable oil*
1 loaf French or Italian bread (about 18 inches long), sliced
    lengthwise
2 tablespoons shredded or grated Parmesan cheese

Substitution: Use ½ cup margarine or butter, melted.

1. Preheat oven to 350°F. Blend savory herb with garlic soup mix and
oil. Brush onto bread, then sprinkle with cheese.

2. Bake 12 minutes or until golden. Slice, then serve.

Makes 1 loaf, about 18 pieces

Broccoli-Cheese Quesadillas

1 cup (4 ounces) shredded fat-free Cheddar cheese
½ cup finely chopped fresh broccoli
2 tablespoons picante sauce or salsa
4 (6- to 7-inch) corn or flour tortillas
1 teaspoon margarine, divided

1. Combine cheese, broccoli and picante sauce in small bowl;
mix well.

2. Spoon one fourth of cheese mixture onto one side of each tortilla;
fold tortilla over filling.

3. Melt ½ teaspoon margarine in 10-inch nonstick skillet over
medium heat. Add 2 quesadillas; cook about 2 minutes on each side
or until tortillas are golden brown and cheese is melted. Repeat with
remaining margarine and quesadillas. Cool completely.

Makes 4 servings

Tip: Refrigerate individually wrapped quesadillas up to 2 days or
freeze up to 3 weeks.

Cheddar Tomato Bacon Toasts

1 jar (16 ounces) RAGÚ® Cheese Creations!® Double Cheddar Sauce
1 medium tomato, chopped
5 slices bacon, crisp-cooked and crumbled (about ⅓ cup)
2 loaves Italian bread (each about 16 inches long), each cut into
    16 slices

1. Preheat oven to 350°F. In medium bowl, combine Ragú® Cheese Creations! Sauce, tomato and bacon.

2. On baking sheet, arrange bread slices. Evenly top with sauce mixture.

3. Bake 10 minutes or until sauce mixture is bubbling. Serve immediately.   *Makes 16 servings*

Prep Time: 10 minutes
Cook Time: 10 minutes

Buffalo-Style Shrimp

⅓ cup *Frank's® RedHot®* Cayenne Pepper Sauce
⅓ cup butter or margarine, melted
1 pound raw large shrimp, shelled and deveined
2 ribs celery, cut into large pieces

1. Combine *Frank's RedHot* Sauce and butter in small bowl. Alternately thread shrimp and celery onto metal skewers. Place in shallow bowl. Pour ⅓ cup *Frank's RedHot* Sauce mixture over kabobs. Cover; refrigerate 30 minutes. Prepare grill.

2. Grill,* over medium coals, 3 to 5 minutes or until shrimp are opaque. Heat remaining *Frank's RedHot* Sauce mixture; pour over shrimp and celery.   *Makes 4 servings*

Or, broil 6 inches from heat.

Prep Time: 10 minutes
Marinate Time: 30 minutes
Cook Time: 5 minutes

Mexican Roll-Ups

6 uncooked lasagna noodles
¾ cup prepared guacamole
¾ cup chunky salsa
¾ cup (3 ounces) shredded fat-free Cheddar cheese
  Additional salsa (optional)

1. Cook lasagna noodles according to package directions, omitting salt. Rinse with cool water; drain. Cool.

2. Spread 2 tablespoons guacamole onto each noodle; top each with 2 tablespoons salsa and 2 tablespoons cheese.

3. Roll up noodles jelly-roll fashion. Cut each roll-up in half to form two equal-size roll-ups. Serve immediately with salsa or cover with plastic wrap and refrigerate up to 3 hours.   *Makes 12 servings*

quick tip

> *To prepare your own guacamole, combine 2 mashed large avocados, ¼ cup finely chopped tomato, 2 tablespoons minced onion, 2 tablespoons lime juice, ½ teaspoon salt and ¼ teaspoon hot pepper sauce. Add black pepper to taste; mix well.*

Mexican Roll-Ups

Hidden Valley Ranch® Cheese Fingers

2 small loaves French bread (8 ounces each), cut in half lengthwise
1 package (8 ounces) cream cheese or Neufchâtel cheese
1 packet (1 ounce) HIDDEN VALLEY® The Original Ranch® Salad
    Dressing & Seasoning Mix
4 cups assorted toppings, such as chopped onions, chopped bell
    peppers and grated cheese

Slice bread crosswise into 1-inch fingers, leaving fingers attached. Mix cream cheese and salad dressing & seasoning mix together. Spread on cut sides of bread. Pile on toppings. Broil until brown and bubbly.

Makes about 4½ dozen fingers

Chili Garlic Prawns

2 tablespoons vegetable oil
1 pound prawns, peeled and deveined
3 tablespoons LEE KUM KEE® Chili Garlic Sauce
1 green onion, cut into slices

1. Heat oil in wok or skillet.

2. Add prawns and stir-fry until just pink.

3. Add chili garlic sauce and stir-fry until prawns are completely cooked.

4. Sprinkle with green onion and serve. *Makes 4 servings*

Roasted Sweet Pepper Tapas

2 red bell peppers (8 ounces each)
1 clove garlic, minced
1 teaspoon chopped fresh oregano *or* ½ teaspoon dried oregano
2 tablespoons olive oil
  Garlic bread (optional)
  Fresh oregano sprig for garnish

1. Cover broiler pan with foil. Adjust rack so that broiler pan is about 4 inches from heat source. Preheat broiler. Place peppers on foil. Broil 15 to 20 minutes until blackened on all sides, turning peppers every 5 minutes with tongs.

2. To steam peppers and loosen skin, place blackened peppers in paper bag. Close bag; set aside to cool about 15 to 20 minutes.

3. To peel peppers, cut around core, twist and remove. Cut peppers in half; place pepper halves on cutting board. Peel off skin with paring knife; rinse under cold water to remove seeds.

4. Lay halves flat and slice lengthwise into ¼-inch strips.

5. Transfer pepper strips to glass jar. Add garlic, oregano and oil. Close lid; shake to blend. Marinate at least 1 hour. Serve on plates with garlic bread or refrigerate in jar up to 1 week. Garnish, if desired.

Makes 6 servings

quick tip

> *Use this roasting technique for all types of sweet and hot peppers. Broiling time will vary depending on size of pepper. When handling hot peppers, such as Anaheim, jalapeño, poblano or serrano, wear plastic disposable gloves and use caution to prevent irritation of skin or eyes. Green bell peppers do not work as well since their skins are thinner.*

Spinach Cheese Bundles

1 container (6½ ounces) garlic and herb-flavored spreadable cheese
½ cup chopped fresh spinach
¼ teaspoon pepper
1 package (17¼ ounces) frozen puff pastry, thawed
   Sweet and sour or favorite dipping sauce (optional)

1. Preheat oven to 400°F. Combine spreadable cheese, spinach and pepper in small bowl; mix well.

2. Roll out one sheet puff pastry dough on floured surface into 12-inch square. Cut into 16 (3-inch) squares. Place about 1 teaspoon cheese mixture in center of each square. Brush edges of squares with water. Bring edges together up over filling and twist tightly to seal; fan out corners of puff pastry.

3. Place bundles 2 inches apart on baking sheet. Bake about 13 minutes or until golden brown. Repeat with remaining sheet of puff pastry and cheese mixture. Serve warm with dipping sauce, if desired.   *Makes 32 bundles*

Baked Apricot Brie

1 round (8 ounce) Brie cheese
⅓ cup apricot preserves
2 tablespoons sliced almonds
    Cracked pepper or other assorted crackers

1. Preheat oven to 400°F. Place cheese in small baking pan; spread top of cheese with preserves and sprinkle with almonds.

2. Bake about 10 to 12 minutes or until cheese begins to melt and lose its shape. Serve hot with crackers. Refrigerate leftovers; reheat before serving. *Makes 6 servings*

Cook Time: 12 minutes

quick tip

> *Brie is a soft-ripened, unpressed cheese made from cow's milk. It has a distinctive round shape, edible white rind and creamy yellow interior. Avoid Brie that has a chalky center (it is underripe) or a strong ammonia odor (it is overripe). The cheese should give slightly to pressure and have an evenly colored, barely moist rind.*

Hot & Spicy Buffalo Chicken Wings

1 can (15 ounces) DEL MONTE® Original Sloppy Joe Sauce
¼ cup thick and chunky salsa, medium
1 tablespoon red wine vinegar or cider vinegar
20 chicken wings (about 4 pounds)

1. Preheat oven to 400°F.

2. Combine sloppy joe sauce, salsa and vinegar in small bowl. Remove ¼ cup sauce mixture to serve with cooked chicken wings; cover and refrigerate. Set aside remaining sauce mixture.

3. Arrange wings in single layer in large, shallow baking pan; brush wings with remaining sauce mixture.

4. Bake chicken, uncovered, on middle rack in oven 35 minutes or until chicken is no longer pink in center, turning and brushing with remaining sauce mixture after 15 minutes. Serve with reserved ¼ cup sauce. Garnish, if desired. *Makes 4 servings*

Prep Time: 5 minutes
Cook Time: 35 minutes

Crostini

¼ loaf whole wheat baguette (4 ounces)
4 plum tomatoes
1 cup (4 ounces) shredded part-skim mozzarella cheese
3 tablespoons prepared pesto sauce
Chopped fresh basil

1. Preheat oven to 400°F. Slice baguette into 16 very thin, diagonal slices. Slice each tomato vertically into four ¼-inch slices.

2. Place baguette slices on nonstick baking sheet. Top each with 1 tablespoon cheese, then 1 slice tomato. Bake about 8 minutes or until bread is lightly toasted and cheese is melted. Remove from oven; top each crostini with about ½ teaspoon pesto sauce. Garnish with fresh basil, if desired. Serve warm. *Makes 8 servings*

BelGioioso® Fontina Melt

1 loaf Italian or French bread
2 fresh tomatoes, cubed
Basil leaves, julienned
BELGIOIOSO® Fontina Cheese, sliced

Cut bread lengthwise into halves. Top each half with tomatoes and sprinkle with basil. Top with BelGioioso Fontina Cheese. Place in oven at 350°F for 10 to 12 minutes or until cheese is golden brown.
Makes 6 to 8 servings

Satisfying
SIDE DISHES

Fast Pesto Focaccia

1 can (10 ounces) pizza crust dough
2 tablespoons prepared pesto
4 sun-dried tomatoes packed in oil, drained

1. Preheat oven to 425°F. Lightly grease 8×8×2-inch pan. Unroll pizza dough; fold in half and pat into pan.

2. Spread pesto evenly over dough. Chop tomatoes or snip with kitchen scissors; sprinkle over pesto. Press tomatoes into dough. Make indentations in dough every 2 inches using wooden spoon handle.

3. Bake 10 to 12 minutes or until golden brown. Cut into squares and serve warm or at room temperature.

Makes 16 squares

Prep and Cook Time: 20 minutes

Herbed Corn on the Cob

1 tablespoon butter or margarine
1 teaspoon mixed dried herb leaves, such as basil, oregano,
    sage and rosemary
⅛ teaspoon salt
    Black pepper
4 ears corn, husks removed

MICROWAVE DIRECTIONS

1. Combine butter, herbs, salt and pepper in small microwavable bowl. Microwave at MEDIUM (50%) 30 to 45 seconds or until butter is melted.

2. With pastry brush, coat corn with butter mixture. Place corn on microwavable plate; microwave at HIGH 5 to 6 minutes. Turn corn over and microwave at HIGH 5 to 6 minutes until tender.

Makes 4 servings

Onion-Roasted Potatoes

1 envelope LIPTON® RECIPE SECRETS® Onion Soup Mix*
4 medium all-purpose potatoes, cut into large chunks (about
    2 pounds)
⅓ cup olive or vegetable oil

*Also terrific with LIPTON® RECIPE SECRETS® Onion Mushroom, Golden Onion or Savory Herb with Garlic Soup Mix.

1. Preheat oven to 450°F. In large plastic bag or bowl, add all ingredients. Close bag and shake, or toss in bowl, until potatoes are evenly coated.

2. In 13×9-inch baking or roasting pan, arrange potatoes; discard bag.

3. Bake uncovered, stirring occasionally, 40 minutes or until potatoes are tender and golden brown. *Makes 4 servings*

Herbed Corn on the Cob

Satisfying Side Dishes

Cottage Fried Potatoes

Canola oil
3 to 4 russet potatoes (about 1½ pounds), cut into wedges
Coarse salt

1. Preheat oven to warm. Line 2 large baking sheets with paper towels; set aside.

2. Pour oil into large deep skillet or wok to 1-inch depth. Attach deep-fry or candy thermometer to side of skillet, making sure bulb is submerged in oil but not touching bottom of skillet. Heat oil over high heat until thermometer registers 390°F.

3. Carefully slide 8 to 10 potato wedges into skillet. (Do not crowd skillet or oil will lose too much heat.) Reduce heat to medium-high; cook about 4 minutes or until potatoes are deep golden brown and skins are crispy, turning gently to separate wedges so that they cook evenly.

4. Carefully remove potatoes and arrange in single layer on baking sheet. Blot excess oil from potatoes. Place baking sheet in oven to keep potatoes warm.

5. Repeat steps 2 through 4 with remaining potatoes. Sprinkle potatoes with salt to taste. Serve hot.　　　　*Makes 4 to 6 servings*

French Onion Bread Stix

1⅓ cups *French's®* **French Fried Onions, crushed**
¼ cup grated Parmesan cheese
1 container (11 ounces) refrigerated soft bread sticks
1 egg white, beaten

1. Preheat oven to 350°F. Combine French Fried Onions and cheese in pie plate. Separate dough into 12 pieces on sheet of waxed paper.

2. Brush one side of dough with egg white. Dip pieces, wet sides down, into onion mixture, pressing firmly. Baste top surface with egg white and dip into onion mixture.

3. Twist pieces to form spirals. Arrange on ungreased baking sheet. Bake 15 to 20 minutes or until golden brown.

Makes 12 bread sticks

Prep Time: 5 minutes
Cook Time: 15 minutes

I-2-3 Cheddar Broccoli Casserole

1 jar (16 ounces) RAGÚ® Cheese Creations!® Double Cheddar Sauce
2 boxes (10 ounces each) frozen broccoli florets, thawed
¼ cup plain or Italian seasoned dry bread crumbs
1 tablespoon margarine or butter, melted

1. Preheat oven to 350°F. In 1½-quart casserole, combine Ragú Cheese Creations! Sauce and broccoli.

2. Evenly top with bread crumbs combined with margarine.

3. Bake uncovered 20 minutes or until bread crumbs are golden and broccoli is tender.   *Makes 6 servings*

Prep Time: 5 minutes
Cook Time: 20 minutes

quick tip

> Substitute your favorite frozen vegetables or vegetable blend for broccoli florets.

1-2-3 Cheddar Broccoli Casserole

Brown Rice Royal

2 cups (about 8 ounces) sliced fresh mushrooms
½ cup thinly sliced green onions
1 tablespoon vegetable oil
3 cups cooked brown rice (cooked in beef broth)

Cook mushrooms and onions in oil in large skillet over medium-high heat until tender. Add rice. Stir until thoroughly heated.

Makes 6 servings

Microwave Directions: Combine mushrooms, onions and oil in 2-quart microproof baking dish. Cook on HIGH (100% power) 2 to 3 minutes. Add rice; continue to cook on HIGH 3 to 4 minutes, stirring after 2 minutes, or until thoroughly heated.

*Favorite recipe from **USA Rice Federation***

Cauliflower with Onion Butter

1 cup (2 sticks) butter, divided
1 cup diced onion
1 head cauliflower, cut into 2½×2-inch florets

1. Melt ½ cup butter in 10-inch skillet over medium heat. Add onion; cook and stir until onion is brown, about 20 minutes.

2. Meanwhile, place cauliflower in microwavable container with ½ cup water. Microwave on HIGH 8 minutes or until crisp-tender.

3. Add remaining butter to skillet with onion; cook and stir until butter is melted. Pour over cooked cauliflower; serve immediately.

Makes 18 (½ cup) servings

Satisfying Side Dishes

Classic Polenta

6 cups water
2 teaspoons salt
2 cups yellow cornmeal
¼ cup vegetable oil

1. Bring water and salt to a boil in large, heavy saucepan over medium-high heat. Stirring water vigorously, add cornmeal in very thin but steady stream (do not let lumps form). Reduce heat to low.

2. Cook polenta, uncovered, 40 to 60 minutes until very thick, stirring frequently. Polenta is ready when spoon will stand upright by itself in center of mixture. Polenta can be served at this point.*

3. For fried polenta, spray 11×7-inch baking pan with nonstick cooking spray. Spread polenta mixture evenly into baking pan. Cover and let stand at room temperature at least 6 hours or until completely cooled and firm.

4. Unmold polenta onto cutting board. Cut polenta crosswise into 1¼-inch-wide strips. Cut strips into 2- to 3-inch-long pieces.

5. Heat oil in large, heavy skillet over medium-high heat; reduce heat to medium. Fry polenta pieces, half at a time, 4 to 5 minutes until golden on all sides, turning as needed. Garnish as desired.

Makes 6 to 8 servings

*Polenta is an important component of Northern Italian cooking. The basic preparation presented here can be served in two forms. Hot freshly made polenta, prepared through step 2, can be mixed with ⅓ cup butter and ⅓ cup grated Parmesan cheese and served as a first course. Or, pour onto a large platter and top with a hearty meat sauce for a main dish. Fried polenta, as prepared here, is appropriate as an appetizer or as a side dish with meat.

Herbed Green Beans

1 pound fresh green beans, stem ends removed
1 teaspoon extra virgin olive oil
2 tablespoons chopped fresh basil *or* **2 teaspoons dried basil**

1. Steam green beans 5 minutes or until crisp-tender. Rinse under cold running water; drain and set aside.

2. Just before serving, heat oil over medium-low heat in large nonstick skillet. Add basil; cook and stir 1 minute, then add green beans. Cook until heated through. Garnish with additional fresh basil, if desired. Serve immediately.   *Makes 6 servings*

quick tip

> *When buying green beans, look for vivid green, crisp beans without scars. Pods should be well shaped and slim with small seeds. Buy beans of uniform size to ensure even cooking, and avoid bruised or large beans.*

Garlic Bread

6 whole heads of garlic
1 teaspoon dried oregano
4½ teaspoons extra virgin olive oil
1 loaf, unsliced, crusty sourdough or French bread, cut
horizontally in half (1½ pounds)
Black pepper

1. Preheat oven to 350°F. Cut tops off heads of garlic and peel each head. Place heads, cut sides up, in small baking pan and sprinkle with oregano. Cover tightly with foil and bake 30 minutes. Uncover and bake 30 minutes more. Remove from oven, cool until easy to handle.

2. Carefully squeeze soft roasted garlic out of each clove to yield about ¾ cup. Place in blender or food processor; add oil and process until smooth.

3. Spread garlic mixture evenly on both halves of bread and sprinkle lightly with black pepper. Place halves together and cut loaf vertically into 8 equal pieces, being careful to keep loaf intact. Wrap tightly in foil. Bake 30 minutes.

4. To serve, unwrap loaf leaving foil crushed around outside to keep warm.   *Makes 16 servings*

Satisfying Side Dishes

Vegetable-Stuffed Baked Potatoes

**1 jar (16 ounces) RAGÚ® Cheese Creations!® Roasted Garlic
   Parmesan Sauce or Double Cheddar Sauce**
1 bag (16 ounces) frozen assorted vegetables, cooked and drained
6 large baking potatoes, unpeeled and baked

In 2-quart saucepan, heat Ragú Cheese Creations! Sauce. Stir in
vegetables; heat through.

Cut a lengthwise slice from top of each potato. Lightly mash pulp in
each potato. Evenly spoon sauce mixture onto each potato. Sprinkle,
if desired, with ground black pepper.   *Makes 6 servings*

Garlic Greens

5 to 6 ounces fresh spinach leaves
1 tablespoon margarine or olive oil
4 cloves garlic, minced

1. Wash spinach; remove and discard stems. Melt margarine in small
skillet over medium heat. Add garlic; cook and stir about 1 minute.
Do not allow garlic to brown.

2. Add spinach to skillet; stir to coat with garlic. Cover; cook 1 minute
or until spinach is wilted. Serve immediately.   *Makes 2 servings*

Vegetable-Stuffed Baked Potato

Satisfying Side Dishes

Honey-Glazed Carrots and Parsnips

½ **pound carrots, thinly sliced**
½ **pound parsnips, peeled and thinly sliced**
¼ **cup chopped fresh parsley**
2 **tablespoons honey**
   Additional fresh parsley (optional)

Steam carrots and parsnips over simmering water in large saucepan 3 to 4 minutes or until crisp-tender. Rinse under cold running water; drain. Combine carrots, parsnips, parsley and honey in same saucepan. Cook over medium heat just until heated through. Garnish with additional parsley, if desired. Serve immediately.

Makes 6 (⅔-cup) servings

Peas with Cukes 'n' Dill

2 **pounds fresh peas***
2 **tablespoons butter or margarine**
½ **medium cucumber, halved, seeded and cut into ¼-inch slices**
1 **teaspoon dried dill weed**
   Salt and pepper
   Fresh dill, pineapple sage leaves and edible flowers, such as pansies, for garnish

*Or, substitute 1 (10-ounce) package frozen peas, thawed, for fresh peas.

1. To prepare peas, press each pea pod between thumbs and forefingers to open.

2. Push peas out with thumb into colander; discard pods. Rinse peas under running water. Drain well; set aside.

3. Heat butter in medium skillet over medium-high heat until melted and bubbly. Cook and stir peas and cucumber in hot butter 5 minutes or until vegetables are crisp-tender.

4. Stir in dill weed; season with salt and pepper to taste. Transfer to warm serving dish. Garnish, if desired. Serve immediately.

Makes 4 servings

Satisfying Side Dishes

Swiss Rosti Potatoes

4 large russet potatoes (about 6 ounces each)*
4 tablespoons butter or margarine
 Salt and pepper
 Cherry tomato wedges and fresh rosemary sprigs for garnish

*Prepare potatoes several hours or up to 1 day in advance.

1. Preheat oven to 400°F. To prepare potatoes, scrub with soft vegetable brush under running water; rinse well. Pierce each potato in several places with fork. Bake 1 hour or until fork-tender. Cool completely, then refrigerate.

2. When potatoes are cold, peel with paring knife. Grate potatoes by hand with large section of metal grater or use food processor with large grater disk.

3. Heat butter in 10-inch skillet over medium-high heat until melted and bubbly. Press grated potatoes evenly into skillet. (Do not stir or turn potatoes.) Season with salt and pepper to taste. Cook 10 to 12 minutes until golden brown.

4. Turn off heat; invert serving plate over skillet. Turn potatoes out onto plate. Garnish, if desired. Serve immediately.

Makes 4 servings

Oven-Roasted Vegetables

1½ pounds assorted cut-up fresh vegetables*
3 tablespoons I CAN'T BELIEVE IT'S NOT BUTTER!® Spread, melted
2 cloves garlic, finely chopped
1 tablespoon chopped fresh oregano leaves *or* 1 teaspoon dried
    oregano leaves, crushed
  Salt and ground black pepper to taste

*Use any combination of the following: zucchini, red, green or yellow bell peppers, Spanish or red onions, white or portobello mushrooms and carrots.

Preheat oven to 450°F.

In bottom of broiler pan, without rack, combine all ingredients. Roast 20 minutes or until vegetables are tender, stirring once.

Makes 4 servings

Oven-Roasted Vegetables

Roasted Idaho & Sweet Potatoes

1 envelope LIPTON® RECIPE SECRETS® Onion Soup Mix
2 medium all-purpose potatoes, peeled, if desired, and cut into
   large chunks (about 1 pound)
2 medium sweet potatoes or yams, peeled, if desired, and cut into
   large chunks (about 1 pound)
¼ cup olive or vegetable oil

1. Preheat oven to 425°F. In large plastic bag or bowl, combine all ingredients. Close bag and shake, or toss in bowl, until potatoes are evenly coated.

2. In 13×9-inch baking or roasting pan, arrange potatoes; discard bag.

3. Bake uncovered, stirring occasionally, 40 minutes or until potatoes are tender and golden.   *Makes 4 servings*

quick tip

Sweet potatoes are a wonderful (and often overlooked) health food—they're fat free, a good source of fiber and a great source of beta-carotene. They are also rich in potassium and vitamin C.

Roasted Idaho & Sweet Potatoes

Tempting
POULTRY

Garlic Mushroom Chicken Melt

**4 boneless, skinless chicken breast halves (about
    1¼ pounds)
1 envelope LIPTON® RECIPE SECRETS® Savory Herb
    with Garlic Soup Mix
1 can (14 ounces) diced tomatoes, undrained *or* 1 large
    tomato, chopped
1 tablespoon olive or vegetable oil
½ cup shredded mozzarella or Monterey Jack cheese
    (about 2 ounces)**

1. Preheat oven to 375°F. In 13×9-inch baking or roasting
pan, arrange chicken. Pour soup mix blended with
tomatoes and oil over chicken.

2. Bake uncovered 25 minutes or until chicken is no longer
pink in center.

3. Sprinkle with mozzarella cheese and bake an additional
2 minutes or until cheese is melted.   *Makes 4 servings*

Herbed Chicken & Vegetables

2 medium all-purpose potatoes, thinly sliced (about 1 pound)
2 medium carrots, sliced
4 bone-in chicken pieces (about 2 pounds)
1 envelope LIPTON® RECIPE SECRETS® Savory Herb with Garlic
   Soup Mix
⅓ cup water
1 tablespoon olive or vegetable oil

1. Preheat oven to 425°F. In broiler pan, without the rack, place potatoes and carrots; arrange chicken on top. Pour soup mix blended with water and oil over chicken and vegetables.

2. Bake uncovered 40 minutes or until chicken is no longer pink and vegetables are tender.   *Makes 4 servings*

Slow Cooker Method: Place all ingredients in slow cooker, arranging chicken on top; cover. Cook on HIGH 4 hours or LOW 6 to 8 hours.

Prep Time: 10 minutes
Cook Time: 40 minutes

Classic Fried Chicken

¾ **cup all-purpose flour**
1 **teaspoon salt**
¼ **teaspoon pepper**
1 **frying chicken (2½ to 3 pounds), cut up, or chicken pieces**
½ **cup CRISCO® Oil***

Use your favorite Crisco Oil product.

1. Combine flour, salt and pepper in paper or plastic bag. Add a few pieces of chicken at a time. Shake to coat.

2. Heat oil to 365°F in electric skillet or on medium-high heat in large heavy skillet. Fry chicken 30 to 40 minutes without lowering heat. Turn once for even browning. Drain on paper towels.

Makes 4 servings

Note: For thicker crust, increase flour to 1½ cups. Shake damp chicken in seasoned flour. Place on waxed paper. Let stand for 5 to 20 minutes before frying.

Spicy Fried Chicken: Increase pepper to ½ teaspoon. Combine pepper with ½ teaspoon poultry seasoning, ½ teaspoon paprika, ½ teaspoon cayenne pepper and ¼ teaspoon dry mustard. Rub on chicken before step 1. Substitute 2¼ teaspoons garlic salt, ¼ teaspoon salt and ¼ teaspoon celery salt for 1 teaspoon salt. Combine with flour in step 1 and proceed as directed above.

Summer Raspberry Chicken

4 boneless, skinless chicken breast halves (about 1 pound), pounded to ¼-inch thickness
¾ cup LAWRY'S® Dijon & Honey Marinade with Lemon Juice, divided
1 cup fresh or frozen raspberries
½ cup walnut pieces

Grill or broil chicken 10 to 15 minutes or until no longer pink in center and juices run clear when cut, turning once and basting often with ½ cup Dijon & Honey Marinade. *Do not baste during last 5 minutes of cooking.* Discard any remaining marinade. Cut chicken into strips. In food processor or blender, process raspberries and additional ¼ cup Dijon & Honey Marinade 10 seconds. Drizzle raspberry sauce over chicken; sprinkle with walnuts.

Makes 4 servings

quick tip

Serve chicken on field greens or angel hair pasta. Garnish with fresh raspberries, if desired.

Summer Raspberry Chicken

Country Herb Roasted Chicken

1 chicken (2½ to 3 pounds), cut into serving pieces (with or without skin) *or* **1½ pounds boneless skinless chicken breast halves**
1 envelope LIPTON® RECIPE SECRETS® Savory Herb with Garlic Soup Mix
2 tablespoons water
1 tablespoon BERTOLLI® Olive Oil

1. Preheat oven to 375°F.

2. In 13×9-inch baking or roasting pan, arrange chicken. In small bowl, combine remaining ingredients; brush on chicken.

3. For chicken pieces, bake uncovered 45 minutes or until chicken is no longer pink. For chicken breast halves, bake uncovered 20 minutes or until chicken is no longer pink.   *Makes about 4 servings*

quick tip

> To make a complete meal, serve this dish with a lettuce and tomato salad, scalloped potatoes and cooked green beans.

Caribbean Jerk Chicken
with Quick Fruit Salsa

**1 cup plus 2 tablespoons LAWRY'S® Caribbean Jerk Marinade with
Papaya Juice, divided
1 can (15¼ ounces) tropical fruit salad, drained
4 boneless, skinless chicken breast halves (about 1 pound)**

In small glass bowl, combine 2 tablespoons Caribbean Jerk Marinade
and tropical fruit; mix well and set aside. In large resealable plastic
food storage bag, combine additional 1 cup Caribbean Jerk Marinade
and chicken; seal bag. Marinate in refrigerator at least 30 minutes.
Remove chicken from marinade; discard used marinade. Grill or broil
chicken until no longer pink in center, about 10 to 15 minutes, turning
halfway through grilling time. Top chicken with fruit salsa.

Makes 4 servings

Serving Suggestion: Serve with hot cooked rice and black beans.

Asian Chicken and Noodles

**1 package (3 ounces) chicken flavor instant ramen noodles
1 bag (16 ounces) BIRDS EYE® frozen Farm Fresh Mixtures Broccoli,
Carrots and Water Chestnuts*
1 tablespoon vegetable oil
1 pound boneless skinless chicken breasts, cut into thin strips
¼ cup stir-fry sauce**

*Or, substitute 1 bag (16 ounces) Birds Eye® frozen Broccoli Cuts.

• Reserve seasoning packet from noodles.

• Bring 2 cups water to boil in large saucepan. Add noodles and
vegetables. Cook 3 minutes, stirring occasionally; drain.

• Meanwhile, heat oil in large nonstick skillet over medium-high heat.
Add chicken; cook and stir until browned, about 8 minutes.

• Stir in noodles, vegetables, stir-fry sauce and reserved seasoning
packet; heat through. *Makes about 4 servings*

Grilled Rosemary Chicken

2 tablespoons lemon juice
2 tablespoons olive oil
2 cloves garlic, minced
2 tablespoons minced fresh rosemary
¼ teaspoon salt
4 boneless skinless chicken breasts

1. Whisk together lemon juice, oil, garlic, rosemary and salt in small bowl. Pour into shallow glass dish. Add chicken, turning to coat both sides with lemon juice mixture. Cover and marinate in refrigerator 15 minutes, turning chicken once.

2. Grill chicken over medium-hot coals 5 to 6 minutes per side or until chicken is no longer pink in center. *Makes 4 servings*

Prep and Cook Time: 30 minutes

quick tip

For added flavor, moisten a few sprigs of fresh rosemary and toss on the hot coals just before grilling.

Grilled Rosemary Chicken

Wish-Bone® Marinade Italiano

¾ cup WISH-BONE® Italian Dressing*
2½ to 3 pounds chicken pieces

*Also terrific with Wish-Bone® Robusto Italian or Just 2 Good Italian Dressing.

In large, shallow nonaluminum baking dish or plastic bag, pour ½ cup Italian dressing over chicken. Cover, or close bag, and marinate in refrigerator, turning occasionally, 3 to 24 hours.

Remove chicken from marinade; discard marinade. Grill or broil chicken, turning once and brushing frequently with remaining ¼ cup dressing, until chicken is no longer pink and juices run clear.

Makes about 4 servings

quick tip

One (2- to 2½-pound) T-bone, boneless sirloin or top loin steak or 6 boneless, skinless chicken breast halves (about 1½ pounds) or 2½ pounds center cut pork chops (about 1 inch thick) may be substituted for chicken pieces.

Tender Baked Chicken

1 chicken (2½ to 3½ pounds), cut into pieces
½ cup HELLMANN'S® or BEST FOODS® Real or Light Mayonnaise
1¼ cups Italian seasoned bread crumbs

1. Brush chicken on all sides with mayonnaise.

2. Place bread crumbs in large plastic food storage bag. Add chicken 1 piece at a time; shake to coat well. Arrange on rack in broiler pan.

3. Bake in 425°F oven about 40 minutes or until golden brown and tender. *Makes 4 servings*

Chicken and Mushrooms with Roasted Garlic Sauce

1 teaspoon olive oil
4 boneless skinless chicken breasts
1 jar (about 28 ounces) roasted garlic pasta sauce
1 cup sliced mushrooms
8 ounces corkscrew pasta, cooked and drained
   Grated fresh Parmesan cheese (optional)

1. Heat olive oil in medium skillet over medium heat. Lightly brown chicken. Remove chicken from skillet and slice into thin strips. Return to skillet.

2. Stir in pasta sauce and mushrooms. Simmer, covered, stirring occasionally, 10 minutes or until chicken is no longer pink in center.

3. Combine pasta and sauce mixture in large bowl. Sprinkle with Parmesan cheese, if desired. *Makes 4 servings*

Cajun Chicken Bayou

2 cups water
1 can (10 ounces) diced tomatoes and green chilies, undrained
1 box UNCLE BEN'S CHEF'S RECIPE™ Traditional Red Beans & Rice
**3 TYSON® Individually Fresh Frozen® Boneless, Skinless Chicken
   Breasts**

COOK: CLEAN: Wash hands. In large skillet, combine water, tomatoes, beans and rice, and contents of seasoning packet; mix well. Add chicken. Bring to a boil. Cover, reduce heat; simmer 30 to 35 minutes or until internal juices of chicken run clear. (Or insert instant-read meat thermometer in thickest part of chicken. Temperature should read 170°F.)

SERVE: Serve with sliced avocados and whole wheat rolls, if desired.

CHILL: Refrigerate leftovers immediately. *Makes 3 servings*

Cook Time: 35 minutes

Crispy Ranch Chicken

1½ cups cornflake crumbs
1 teaspoon dried rosemary
½ teaspoon salt
½ teaspoon black pepper
1½ cups ranch salad dressing
3 pounds chicken pieces (breasts, legs, thighs)

1. Preheat oven to 375°F. Combine cornflakes, rosemary, salt and pepper in medium bowl.

2. Pour salad dressing in separate medium bowl. Dip chicken pieces in salad dressing, coating well. Dredge coated chicken in crumb mixture.

3. Place in 13×9-inch baking dish coated with nonstick cooking spray. Bake 50 to 55 minutes or until juices run clear. Serve with desired side dishes. *Makes 6 servings*

quick tip

> To add an Italian flair to this dish, try substituting 1½ cups Italian-seasoned dried bread crumbs and ½ cup grated Parmesan cheese for the cornflake crumbs, rosemary, salt and pepper. Prepare recipe as directed.

Maple-Glazed Turkey Breast

1 bone-in turkey breast (5 to 6 pounds)
   Roast rack (optional)
¼ cup pure maple syrup
 2 tablespoons butter or margarine, melted
 1 tablespoon bourbon (optional)
 2 teaspoons freshly grated orange peel
   Fresh bay leaves for garnish

1. Prepare barbecue grill with rectangular foil drip pan. Bank briquets on either side of drip pan for indirect cooking.

2. Insert meat thermometer into center of thickest part of turkey breast, not touching bone. Place turkey, bone side down, on roast rack or directly on grid, directly over drip pan. Grill turkey, on covered grill, over medium coals 55 minutes, adding 4 to 9 briquets to both sides of fire after 45 minutes to maintain medium coals.

3. Combine maple syrup, butter, bourbon and orange peel in small bowl; brush half of mixture over turkey. Continue to grill, covered, 10 minutes. Brush with remaining mixture; continue to grill, covered, about 10 minutes or until thermometer registers 170°F.

4. Transfer turkey to carving board; tent with foil. Let stand 10 minutes before carving. Cut turkey into thin slices. Garnish, if desired. *Makes 6 to 8 servings*

Variation: For hickory-smoked flavor, cover 2 cups hickory chips with cold water; soak 20 minutes. Drain; sprinkle over coals just before placing turkey on grid.

Maple-Glazed Turkey Breast

Roasted Chicken au Jus

1 envelope LIPTON® RECIPE SECRETS® Garlic Mushroom Soup Mix*
2 tablespoons olive or vegetable oil
1 (2½- to 3-pound) chicken, cut into serving pieces
½ cup hot water

*Also terrific with LIPTON® RECIPE SECRETS® Savory Herb with Garlic Soup Mix.

1. Preheat oven to 425°F. In large bowl, combine soup mix and oil; add chicken and toss until evenly coated.

2. In bottom of broiler pan without rack, arrange chicken. Roast chicken, basting occasionally, 40 minutes or until chicken is no longer pink.

3. Remove chicken to serving platter. Add hot water to pan and stir, scraping brown bits from bottom of pan. Serve sauce over chicken.

Makes 4 servings

One-Dish Meal

2 bags SUCCESS® Rice
Vegetable cooking spray
1 cup cubed cooked turkey-ham*
1 cup (4 ounces) shredded low-fat Cheddar cheese
1 cup peas

*Or, use cooked turkey, ham or turkey franks.

Prepare rice according to package directions.

Spray 1 quart microwave-safe dish with cooking spray; set aside. Place rice in medium bowl. Add ham, cheese and peas; mix lightly. Spoon into prepared dish; smooth into even layer with spoon. Microwave on HIGH 1 minute; stir. Microwave 30 seconds or until thoroughly heated.

Makes 4 servings

Conventional Oven Directions: Assemble casserole as directed. Spoon into ovenproof 1 quart baking dish sprayed with vegetable cooking spray. Bake at 350°F until thoroughly heated, about 15 to 20 minutes.

Peppery Turkey Fillets

1 package (about ¾ pound) PERDUE® FIT 'N EASY® Fresh Skinless & Boneless Turkey Breast Fillets
¼ cup Worcestershire sauce
1 tablespoon Dijon mustard
1 tablespoon canola oil
2 teaspoons cracked black pepper
Salt

Place fillets in shallow baking dish. In small bowl, combine Worcestershire sauce, mustard and oil. Add fillets to marinade, turning to coat well. Cover and refrigerate 1 hour or longer.

Prepare lightly greased grill for cooking. Remove fillets from marinade; sprinkle with pepper and salt to taste. Grill, uncovered, 5 to 6 inches over medium-hot coals 3 to 5 minutes on each side until cooked through. *Makes 3 to 4 servings*

quick tip

If possible, use a pepper grinder or mortar and pestle to grind pepper as you need it for cooking—the taste is far superior to that of preground pepper, which loses its flavor very quickly.

Cutlets Milanese

**1 package (about 1 pound) PERDUE® FIT 'N EASY® Fresh
  Thin-Sliced Turkey or Chicken Breast Cutlets
  Salt and ground pepper to taste**
½ cup Italian seasoned bread crumbs
½ cup grated Parmesan cheese
1 large egg beaten with 1 teaspoon water
2 to 3 tablespoons olive oil

Season cutlets with salt and pepper. On wax paper, combine bread
crumbs and Parmesan cheese. Dip cutlets in egg mixture and roll in
bread crumb mixture. In large, nonstick skillet over medium-high heat,
heat oil. Add cutlets and sauté 3 minutes per side, until golden brown
and cooked through. *Makes 4 servings*

Prep Time: 6 to 8 minutes
Cook Time: 6 minutes

Enticing
BEEF

Cheesy Spinach Burgers

1 envelope LIPTON® RECIPE SECRETS® Onion Soup Mix
2 pounds ground beef
1 package (10 ounces) frozen chopped spinach, thawed
    and squeezed dry
1 cup shredded mozzarella or Cheddar cheese (about
    4 ounces)

1. In large bowl, combine all ingredients; shape into 8 patties.

2. Grill or broil until done. Serve, if desired, on hamburger buns.
Makes 8 servings

quick tip

> To perk up your burgers, serve them on something
> besides a bun. Try bagels, English muffins, pita bread
> or even tortillas for a fun change of pace!

Prime Rib

3 cloves garlic, minced
1 teaspoon black pepper
1 (3-rib) standing beef roast, trimmed* (about 6 to 7 pounds)

*Ask meat retailer to remove chine bone for easier carving. Fat should be trimmed to ¼-inch thickness.

1. Preheat oven to 450°F.

2. Combine garlic and pepper; rub over all surfaces of roast. Place roast, bone side down, in shallow roasting pan. Insert meat thermometer into thickest part of roast not touching bone or fat.

3. Roast in oven 15 minutes. *Reduce oven temperature to 325°F.* Roast 20 minutes per pound for medium or until internal temperature reaches 145°F when tested with meat thermometer inserted into thickest part of roast, not touching bone. Transfer roast to cutting board; cover with foil.

4. Let stand 15 to 20 minutes to allow for easier carving. Internal temperature will continue to rise 5° to 10°F during stand time. Carve; serve immediately. Garnish as desired.   *Makes 6 to 8 servings*

Enticing Beef

Souper Stuffed Cheese Burgers

1 envelope LIPTON® RECIPE SECRETS® Onion Soup Mix*
2 pounds ground beef
½ cup water
¾ cup shredded Cheddar, mozzarella or Monterey Jack cheese
    (about 6 ounces)

**Also terrific with LIPTON® RECIPE SECRETS® Savory Herb with Garlic, Onion
Mushroom or Beefy Onion Soup Mix.*

1. In large bowl, combine soup mix, ground beef and water; shape
into 12 patties.

2. Place 2 tablespoons cheese in center of 6 patties. Top with
remaining patties and seal edges tightly.

3. Grill or broil until done. Serve, if desired, on onion poppy
seed rolls.   *Makes 6 servings*

Beefy Mac & Double Cheddar

½ pound ground beef
3½ cups water
2 cups elbow macaroni
1 jar (16 ounces) RAGÚ® Cheese Creations!® Double Cheddar Sauce

In 12-inch skillet, brown ground beef; drain. Remove from skillet and set aside.

In same skillet, bring water to a boil over high heat. Stir in macaroni and cook 6 minutes or until tender; do not drain. Return ground beef to skillet. Stir in Ragú Cheese Creations! Sauce; heat through. Season, if desired, with salt and ground black pepper.   *Makes 4 servings*

Cheeseburger Soup

½ **pound ground beef**
3½ **cups water**
½ **cup cherry tomato halves or chopped tomato**
1 **pouch LIPTON® Soup Secrets Ring-O-Noodle Soup Mix**
   with Real Chicken Broth
4 **ounces Cheddar cheese, shredded**

Shape ground beef into 16 mini burgers.

In large saucepan, thoroughly brown burgers; drain. Add water, tomatoes and soup mix; bring to a boil. Reduce heat and simmer uncovered, stirring occasionally, 5 minutes or until burgers are cooked and noodles are tender. Stir in cheese.

Makes about 4 (1-cup) servings

Marinated Flank Steak with Pineapple

1 can (15¼ ounces) DEL MONTE® Sliced Pineapple In Its Own Juice
¼ cup teriyaki sauce
2 tablespoons honey
1 pound flank steak

1. Drain pineapple, reserving 2 tablespoons juice. Set aside pineapple for later use.

2. Combine reserved juice, teriyaki sauce and honey in shallow 2-quart dish; mix well. Add meat; turn to coat. Cover and refrigerate at least 30 minutes or overnight.

3. Remove meat from marinade, reserving marinade. Grill meat over hot coals (or broil), brushing occasionally with reserved marinade. Cook about 4 minutes on each side for rare, about 5 minutes on each side for medium, or about 6 minutes on each side for well done. During last 4 minutes of cooking, brush pineapple slices with marinade; grill until heated through.

4. Slice meat across grain; serve with pineapple. Garnish, if desired.

Makes 4 servings

Note: Marinade that has come into contact with raw meat must be discarded or boiled for several minutes before serving with cooked food.

Prep and Marinate Time: 35 minutes
Cook Time: 10 minutes

Marinated Flank Steak with Pineapple

Ultimate The Original Ranch® Cheese Burgers

**1 packet (1 ounce) HIDDEN VALLEY® The Original Ranch®
    Seasoning & Salad Dressing Mix
1 pound ground beef
1 cup (4 ounces) shredded Cheddar cheese
4 large hamburger buns, toasted**

Combine dressing mix with beef and cheese. Shape into 4 patties; cook thoroughly until no longer pink in center. Serve on toasted buns.

Makes 4 servings

quick tip

Grilling is a great way to cook these burgers. To minimize food sticking to the grid and to assist in the cleanup, grease grill grid with oil or cooking spray before use. However, do not spray the grid over the fire as this could cause a flare-up.

Stir-Fried Beef & Spinach

Nonstick cooking spray
5 ounces fresh spinach leaves, torn
Dash salt
8 ounces top sirloin steak, thinly sliced
¼ cup stir-fry sauce
1 teaspoon sugar
½ teaspoon curry powder
¼ teaspoon ground ginger

1. Coat 12-inch nonstick skillet with cooking spray. Heat skillet over high heat until hot. Add spinach; stir-fry 1 minute or until limp.

2. Remove skillet from heat; transfer spinach to serving platter, sprinkle with salt and cover to keep warm.

3. Wipe out skillet with paper towel. Coat skillet with cooking spray. Heat over high heat until hot. Add beef; stir-fry 1 minute until no longer pink. Add sauce, sugar, curry powder and ginger; cook and stir 1½ minutes or until sauce thickly coats beef.

4. Spoon beef mixture onto spinach.   *Makes 2 servings*

Steakhouse London Broil

1 package KNORR® Recipe Classics™ Roasted Garlic Herb or French Onion Soup, Dip and Recipe Mix
⅓ cup vegetable or olive oil
2 tablespoons red wine vinegar
1 (1½- to 2-pound) beef round steak (for London Broil) or flank steak

• In large plastic food bag or 13×9-inch glass baking dish, blend recipe mix, oil and vinegar.

• Add steak, turning to coat. Close bag, or cover, and marinate in refrigerator 30 minutes to 3 hours.

• Remove meat from marinade, discarding marinade. Grill or broil, turning occasionally, until desired doneness.

• Slice meat thinly across the grain.   *Makes 6 to 8 servings*

Prep Time: 5 minutes
Marinate Time: 30 minutes to 3 hours
Grill Time: 20 minutes

Steakhouse London Broil

Skillet Pasta Dinner

1 pound ground beef
1 jar (26 to 28 ounces) RAGÚ® Robusto! Pasta Sauce
8 ounces rotini pasta, cooked and drained
1 cup shredded cheddar or Monterey Jack cheese, divided
2 teaspoons chili powder (optional)

In 12-inch skillet, brown ground beef over medium-high heat; drain. Stir in Ragú Robusto! Pasta Sauce, hot pasta, ¾ cup cheese and chili powder. Simmer uncovered, stirring occasionally, 5 minutes or until heated through. Sprinkle with remaining ¼ cup cheese.

Makes 4 servings

Enticing Beef

Smothered Steak

    4 to 6 beef cubed steaks (about 1½ to 2 pounds)
      All-purpose flour
    1 can (10¾ ounces) condensed cream of mushroom soup, undiluted
    1 package (1 ounce) dry onion soup mix
      Hot cooked rice (optional)

SLOW COOKER DIRECTIONS

1. Dust steaks lightly with flour. Place in slow cooker.

2. Combine mushroom soup and onion soup mix in medium bowl. Pour over steak. Cover; cook on LOW 6 to 8 hours. Serve over rice, if desired.
          Makes 4 servings

Oriental Beef Kabobs

    1 tablespoon olive oil
    1 tablespoon seasoned rice vinegar
    1 tablespoon soy sauce
    4 purchased beef kabobs

1. Preheat broiler.

2. Whisk together oil, vinegar and soy sauce; brush on kabobs.

3. Arrange kabobs on broiler rack. Broil, 4 inches from heat source, 10 minutes or to desired doneness, turning after 5 minutes.
          Makes 4 servings

Fragrant Beef
with Garlic Sauce

  1 boneless beef top sirloin steak, cut 1 inch thick
      (about 1¼ pounds)
  ⅓ cup teriyaki sauce
10 large cloves garlic, peeled
  ½ cup beef broth
  4 cups hot cooked white rice (optional)

1. Place beef in large plastic bag. Pour teriyaki sauce over beef. Close bag securely; turn to coat. Marinate in refrigerator at least 30 minutes or up to 4 hours.

2. Combine garlic and broth in small saucepan. Bring to a boil over high heat. Reduce heat to medium. Simmer, uncovered, 5 minutes. Cover and simmer 8 to 9 minutes until garlic is softened. Transfer to blender or food processor; process until smooth.

3. Meanwhile, drain beef; reserve marinade. Place beef on rack of broiler pan. Brush with reserved marinade. Broil 5 to 6 inches from heat 5 minutes. Turn beef over; broil 5 minutes more.*

4. Slice beef thinly; serve with garlic sauce and rice, if desired.

Makes 4 servings

*Broiling time is for medium-rare doneness. Adjust time for desired doneness.

Blue Cheese Burgers

1¼ **pounds lean ground beef**
  1 **tablespoon finely chopped onion**
1½ **teaspoons chopped fresh thyme** *or* ½ **teaspoon dried thyme**
 ¾ **teaspoon salt**
   Dash ground pepper
  4 **ounces blue cheese, crumbled**

1. Preheat grill.

2. Combine ground beef, onion, thyme, salt and pepper in medium bowl; mix lightly. Shape into eight patties.

3. Place cheese in center of four patties to within ½ inch of outer edge; top with remaining burgers. Press edges together to seal.

4. Grill 8 minutes or to desired doneness, turning once. Serve with lettuce, tomatoes and Dijon mustard on whole wheat buns, if desired.

Makes 4 servings

Phenomenal
PORK

Grilled Sherry Pork Chops

¼ cup **HOLLAND HOUSE® Sherry Cooking Wine**
¼ cup **GRANDMA'S® Molasses**
2 tablespoons **soy sauce**
4 **pork chops (1 inch thick)**

In plastic bowl, combine sherry, molasses and soy sauce; pour over pork chops. Cover; refrigerate 30 minutes. Prepare grill. Drain pork chops; save marinade. Grill pork chops over medium-high heat 20 to 30 minutes or until pork is no longer pink in center, turning once and brushing frequently with marinade.* Discard any remaining marinade.   *Makes 4 servings*

Do not baste during last 5 minutes of grilling.

Italian-Style Country Pork Ribs

2 tablespoons vegetable oil
2 pounds boneless pork loin country-style ribs*, cut into 3-rib portions
1 jar (32 ounces) spaghetti sauce
1 pound pasta (any variety), cooked and drained
   Grated Parmesan cheese

*Ask your butcher for this cut or substitute boneless pork sirloin chops.

SLOW COOKER DIRECTIONS

1. Heat oil in large skillet over medium-high heat. Add ribs in batches and cook until browned (about 4 to 5 minutes), then turn over and brown other side. Do not crowd pan. Transfer browned ribs to slow cooker and repeat with remaining ribs.

2. Add spaghetti sauce to slow cooker. Cover; cook on LOW 6 to 8 hours, or until meat is tender.

3. Add pasta to slow cooker 10 minutes before serving. Serve pasta and ribs garnished with Parmesan cheese.   *Makes 4 servings*

Lean Homemade Sausage

1 pound lean ground pork
½ **teaspoon dried rosemary**
⅛ **teaspoon salt**
⅛ **teaspoon dried thyme**
⅛ **teaspoon dried marjoram, crushed**
⅛ **teaspoon pepper**

Combine all ingredients; mix well. Place in an air-tight container. Refrigerate 4 to 24 hours to allow flavors to blend.

Shape into ½-inch-thick patties. Cook patties in large skillet over medium heat 4 to 5 minutes on each side or until done. Or, place patties on unheated rack in broiler pan. Broil 5 inches from heat about 5 minutes on each side. *Makes 8 servings*

Prep Time: 10 minutes
Cook Time: 10 minutes

Favorite recipe from National Pork Board

Pork Chops
with Balsamic Vinegar

2 boneless center pork loin chops, 1½ inch thick
1½ teaspoons lemon pepper
1 teaspoon vegetable oil
3 tablespoons balsamic vinegar
2 tablespoons chicken broth
2 teaspoons butter

Pat chops dry. Coat with lemon pepper. Heat oil in heavy skillet over medium-high heat. Add chops. Brown on first side 8 minutes; turn and cook 7 minutes more or until done. Remove from pan and keep warm. Add vinegar and broth to skillet; cook, stirring, until syrupy (about 1 to 2 minutes). Stir in butter until blended. Spoon sauce over chops.

Makes 2 servings

Prep Time: 20 minutes

Favorite recipe from National Pork Board

Pork Chop with Balsamic Vinegar

Marinated Pork Roast

½ cup GRANDMA'S® Molasses
½ cup Dijon mustard
¼ cup tarragon vinegar
   Boneless pork loin roast (3 to 4 pounds)

1. In large plastic bowl, combine molasses, mustard and tarragon vinegar; mix well. Add pork to molasses mixture, turning to coat all sides. Marinate, covered, 1 to 2 hours at room temperature or overnight in refrigerator, turning several times.

2. Heat oven to 325°F. Remove pork from marinade; reserve marinade. Place pork in shallow roasting pan. Cook for 1 to 2 hours or until meat thermometer inserted into thickest part of roast reaches 160°F, basting with marinade* every 30 minutes; discard remaining marinade. Slice roast and garnish, if desired.

Makes 6 to 8 servings

*Do not baste during last 5 minutes of cooking.

Marinated Pork Roast

Peachy Pork Picante

4 boneless top loin pork chops, cubed
2 tablespoons taco seasoning
1 cup salsa
4 tablespoons peach preserves

Toss pork with taco seasoning. Lightly brown pork in a nonstick skillet over medium-high heat; stir in salsa and preserves. Bring to a boil, lower heat. Cover and simmer 8 to 10 minutes.   *Makes 4 servings*

Favorite recipe from National Pork Board

Peppered Pork Tenderloin

1 pork tenderloin, about 1 pound
2 teaspoons lemon pepper
½ teaspoon cayenne (red pepper) or pepper blend seasoning

Rub tenderloin all over with combined peppers; place in shallow roasting pan and roast in 425°F oven for 15 to 20 minutes, until internal temperature (measured with a meat thermometer) reads 155° to 160°F. Let roast rest for 5 minutes before slicing.
Makes 4 servings

Favorite recipe from National Pork Board

Orange Mustard Ham Kabobs

¾ cup honey mustard barbecue sauce
½ cup orange marmalade
1½ pounds CURE 81® ham, cut into 1-inch cubes
2 small oranges, cut into 6 wedges each

In small bowl, combine barbecue sauce and marmalade; mix well. Remove ½ cup mixture for basting; reserve remaining mixture. Thread ham and orange wedges on skewers. Brush with ½ cup barbecue sauce mixture reserved for basting. Grill over medium-hot coals 10 minutes or until browned, turning frequently and basting with remaining barbecue mixture. Serve with reserved sauce mixture.

Makes 6 servings

quick tip

Orange Mustard Ham Kabobs may be broiled 6 inches from heat source for 10 minutes or until browned.

Onion-Baked Pork Chops

1 envelope LIPTON® RECIPE SECRETS® Golden Onion Soup Mix*
⅓ cup plain dry bread crumbs
4 pork chops, 1 inch thick (about 3 pounds)
1 egg, well beaten

*Also terrific with LIPTON® RECIPE SECRETS® Onion or Savory Herb with Garlic Soup Mix.

1. Preheat oven to 400°F. In small bowl, combine soup mix and bread crumbs. Dip chops in egg, then bread crumb mixture, until evenly coated.

2. In lightly greased 13×9-inch baking or roasting pan, arrange chops.

3. Bake uncovered 20 minutes or until barely pink in center, turning once.   *Makes 4 servings*

quick tip

Serve this dish with a side of steamed vegetables, such as zucchini or carrots.

Lemon-Capered Pork Tenderloin

1½ pounds boneless pork tenderloin
1 tablespoon crushed capers
1 teaspoon dried rosemary
⅛ teaspoon black pepper
1 cup water
¼ cup lemon juice

1. Preheat oven to 350°F. Trim fat from tenderloin; discard. Set tenderloin aside.

2. Combine capers, rosemary and black pepper in small bowl. Rub rosemary mixture over tenderloin. Place tenderloin in shallow roasting pan. Pour water and lemon juice over tenderloin.

3. Bake, uncovered, 1 hour or until thermometer inserted in thickest part of tenderloin registers 170°F. Remove from oven; cover with foil. Allow to stand 10 minutes before serving. Garnish as desired.

Makes 8 servings

Barbecue Pork Skillet

4 top loin pork chops
¼ cup low-fat Italian dressing
¼ cup barbecue sauce
1 teaspoon chili powder

In large nonstick skillet, brown pork chops on one side over medium-high heat. Turn chops and add remaining ingredients to pan, stirring to blend. Cover and simmer for 5 to 8 minutes.   *Makes 4 servings*

Favorite recipe from National Pork Board

Cure 81® Ham with Honey Mustard Glaze

1 CURE 81® half ham
1 cup packed brown sugar
½ cup honey
2 tablespoons prepared mustard

Bake ham according to package directions. Meanwhile, combine brown sugar, honey and mustard. Thirty minutes before ham is done, remove from oven. Score surface; spoon on glaze. Return to oven. Continue basting with glaze during last 30 minutes of baking.

Makes 8 to 10 servings

Phenomenal Pork

Garlic Pork Chops

6 bone-in pork chops, ¾ inch thick
1 envelope LIPTON® RECIPE SECRETS® Savory Herb with Garlic
**   Soup Mix**
2 tablespoons vegetable oil
½ cup hot water

1. Preheat oven to 425°F. In broiler pan, without the rack, arrange chops. Brush both sides of chops with soup mix combined with oil.

2. Bake chops 25 minutes or until barely pink in center.

3. Remove chops to serving platter. Add hot water to pan and stir, scraping brown bits from bottom of pan. Serve sauce over chops.

Makes 4 servings

Prep Time: 5 minutes
Cook Time: 25 minutes

Phenomenal Pork

Pleasing
Fish & Shellfish

Hidden Valley® Broiled Fish

**1 packet (1 ounce) HIDDEN VALLEY® The Original Ranch®
Salad Dressing & Seasoning Mix**
⅓ cup lemon juice
3 tablespoons olive oil
3 tablespoons dry white wine or water
**1½ to 2 pounds mild white fish fillets, such as red snapper
or sole**

Combine salad dressing & seasoning mix, lemon juice, olive oil and wine in a shallow dish; mix well. Add fish and coat all sides with mixture. Cover and refrigerate for 15 to 30 minutes. Remove fish from marinade and place on broiler pan. Broil 9 to 12 minutes or until fish begins to flake when tested with a fork.   *Makes 4 servings*

Summer Vegetable & Fish Bundles

4 fish fillets (about 1 pound)
1 pound thinly sliced vegetables*
1 envelope LIPTON® RECIPE SECRETS® Savory Herb with Garlic or
    Golden Onion Soup Mix
½ cup water

Use any combination of the following: thinly sliced mushrooms, zucchini, yellow squash or tomatoes.

On two 18×18-inch pieces heavy-duty aluminum foil, divide fish equally; top with vegetables. Evenly pour savory herb with garlic soup mix blended with water over fish. Wrap foil loosely around fillets and vegetables, sealing edges airtight with double fold. Grill or broil seam side up 15 minutes or until fish flakes.   *Makes about 4 servings*

quick tip

> Serve this dish over hot cooked rice with Lipton® Iced Tea
> mixed with a splash of cranberry juice cocktail.

Pan Seared Halibut Steaks
with Avocado Salsa

4 tablespoons chipotle salsa, divided
½ teaspoon salt, divided
4 small (4 to 5 ounces) *or* 2 large (8 to 10 ounces) halibut steaks,
   cut ¾ inch thick
½ cup diced tomato
½ ripe avocado, diced
2 tablespoons chopped cilantro (optional)
   Lime wedges (optional)

1. Combine 2 tablespoons salsa and ¼ teaspoon salt; spread over both sides of halibut.

2. Heat large nonstick skillet over medium heat until hot. Add halibut; cook 4 to 5 minutes per side or until fish is opaque in center.

3. Meanwhile, combine remaining 2 tablespoons salsa, ¼ teaspoon salt, tomato, avocado and cilantro, if desired, in small bowl. Mix well and spoon over cooked fish. Garnish with lime wedges, if desired.

Makes 4 servings

Poached Seafood Italiano

1 tablespoon olive or vegetable oil
1 large clove garlic, minced
¼ cup dry white wine or chicken broth
4 (6-ounce) salmon steaks or fillets
1 can (14.5 ounces) CONTADINA® Recipe Ready Diced Tomatoes
    with Italian Herbs, undrained
2 tablespoons chopped fresh basil (optional)

1. Heat oil in large skillet. Add garlic; sauté 30 seconds. Add wine. Bring to boil.

2. Add salmon; cover. Reduce heat to medium; simmer 6 minutes.

3. Add undrained tomatoes; simmer 2 minutes or until salmon flakes easily when tested with fork. Sprinkle with basil just before serving, if desired. *Makes 4 servings*

Salmon on a Bed of Leeks

3 to 4 leeks
2 teaspoons butter or margarine
½ cup dry white wine or vermouth
2 salmon fillets (6 to 8 ounces)
  Salt and black pepper to taste
2 tablespoons grated Gruyère cheese

Trim green tops and root ends from leeks; cut lengthwise into quarters, leaving ⅓ inch together at root end. Separate sections. Rinse under cold running water; drain well.

In 10-inch skillet, melt butter over medium heat. Add leeks; cook 2 to 3 minutes, stirring often, until leeks are wilted. Stir in wine; arrange salmon on leeks. Sprinkle with salt and pepper. Reduce heat to low. Cover; cook 5 minutes. Sprinkle cheese over salmon. Cover; cook another 3 to 5 minutes or until salmon is firm and opaque around edges and cheese is melted. Transfer to warm dinner plate with broad spatula; serve immediately.   *Makes 2 servings*

*Favorite recipe from **National Fisheries Institute***

Lobster Tails with Tasty Butters

Scallion Butter or Chili-Mustard Butter (recipes follow)
4 fresh or thawed frozen lobster tails (about 5 ounces each)

1. Prepare grill for direct cooking. Prepare one butter mixture.

2. Rinse lobster tails in cold water. Butterfly tails by cutting lengthwise through centers of hard top shells and meat. Cut to, but not through, bottoms of shells. Press shell halves of tails apart with fingers. Brush lobster meat with butter mixture.

3. Place tails on grid, meat side down. Grill over medium-high heat 4 minutes. Turn tails meat side up. Brush with butter mixture and grill 4 to 5 minutes or until lobster meat turns opaque.

4. Heat remaining butter mixture, stirring occasionally. Serve lobster with butter sauce for dipping. *Makes 4 servings*

Tasty Butters

SCALLION BUTTER
   ⅓ **cup butter or margarine, melted**
   1 **tablespoon finely chopped green onion tops**
   1 **tablespoon lemon juice**
   1 **teaspoon grated lemon peel**
   ¼ **teaspoon black pepper**

CHILI-MUSTARD BUTTER
   ⅓ **cup butter or margarine, melted**
   1 **tablespoon chopped onion**
   1 **tablespoon Dijon mustard**
   1 **teaspoon chili powder**

For each butter sauce, combine ingredients in small bowl.

Lobster Tail with Chili-Mustard Butter

Nutty Pan-Fried Trout

2 tablespoons oil
4 trout fillets (about 6 ounces each)
½ cup seasoned bread crumbs
½ cup pine nuts

1. Heat oil in large skillet over medium heat. Lightly coat fish with crumbs. Add to skillet.

2. Cook 8 minutes or until fish flakes easily when tested with fork, turning after 5 minutes. Remove fish from skillet. Place on serving platter; keep warm.

3. Add pine nuts to drippings in skillet. Cook and stir 3 minutes or until pine nuts are lightly toasted. Sprinkle over fish.

Makes 4 servings

quick tip

Trout fillets can be sprinkled with other toasted nuts, such as almonds, pecans or walnuts.

Creamy Garlic Clam Sauce with Linguine

1 jar (16 ounces) RAGÚ® Cheese Creations!® Roasted Garlic Parmesan Sauce
2 cans (6½ ounces each) chopped clams, undrained
1 tablespoon chopped fresh parsley *or* **½ teaspoon dried parsley flakes**
8 ounces linguine or spaghetti, cooked and drained

1. In 3-quart saucepan, cook Ragú Cheese Creations! Sauce, clams and parsley over medium heat, stirring occasionally, 10 minutes.

2. Serve over hot linguine and garnish, if desired, with fresh lemon wedges.   *Makes 4 servings*

Prep Time: 5 minutes
Cook Time: 15 minutes

Pleasing Fish & Shellfish

Sweet & Zesty Fish
with Fruit Salsa

¼ cup *French's®* Zesty Deli Mustard
¼ cup honey
2 cups chopped assorted fresh fruit (pineapple, kiwi, strawberries and mango)
1 pound sea bass or cod fillets or other firm-fleshed white fish

1. Preheat broiler or grill. Combine mustard and honey. Stir *2 tablespoons* mustard mixture into fruit; set aside.

2. Brush remaining mustard mixture on both sides of fillets. Place in foil-lined broiler pan. Broil (or grill) fish 6 inches from heat for 8 minutes or until fish is opaque.

3. Serve fruit salsa with fish.   *Makes 4 servings*

Tip: To prepare this meal even faster, purchase cut-up fresh fruit from the salad bar.

Prep Time: 15 minutes
Cook Time: 8 minutes

Sweet & Zesty Fish with Fruit Salsa

Fried Orange Shrimp

1 cup all-purpose flour
1 cup Florida orange juice
1 Florida egg, beaten
½ teaspoon salt
   Oil for deep frying
1½ pounds raw Florida shrimp, peeled and deveined

Combine flour, orange juice, egg and salt; mix well. Heat oil in large skillet to 350°F. Dip shrimp into batter to coat, then place in oil to fry. Cook shrimp about 1 minute or until golden brown. Remove from oil and drain on paper towels. *Makes 6 servings*

Favorite recipe from **Florida Department of Agriculture and Consumer Services, Bureau of Seafood and Aquaculture**

quick tip

If possible, use a deep-fat thermometer when deep frying. If one is not available, drop a cube of white bread in the hot oil. The bread will brown evenly in 1 minute at approximately 360° to 365°F, 40 seconds at 365° to 370°F, and 20 seconds at 370° to 375°F.

Dilled Salmon in Parchment

2 skinless salmon fillets (4 to 6 ounces each)
2 tablespoons butter or margarine, melted
1 tablespoon lemon juice
1 tablespoon chopped fresh dill
1 tablespoon chopped shallots

1. Preheat oven to 400°F. Cut 2 pieces parchment paper into 12-inch squares; fold squares in half diagonally and cut into half heart shapes. Open parchment; place fish fillet on one side of each heart.

2. Combine butter and lemon juice in small cup; drizzle over fish. Sprinkle with dill, shallots and salt and pepper to taste.

3. Fold parchment hearts in half. Beginning at top of heart, fold edges together, 2 inches at a time. At tip of heart, fold parchment over to seal.

4. Bake fish about 10 minutes or until parchment pouch puffs up. To serve, cut an "X" through top layer of parchment and fold back points to display contents. *Makes 2 servings*

Prep and Cook Time: 20 minutes

Pleasing Fish & Shellfish

Dashing
DESSERTS

Dessert Grape Clusters

2 pounds seedless red and/or green grapes
1 pound premium white chocolate, coarsely chopped
2 cups finely chopped honey-roasted cashews
   Grape leaves for garnish

1. Rinse grapes under cold running water in colander; drain well. Cut grapes into clusters of 3 grapes with kitchen shears. Place clusters in single layer on paper towels. Let stand at room temperature until completely dry.

2. Melt chocolate in top of double boiler over hot, not boiling, water. Stir until chocolate is melted. Remove from heat.

3. Place cashews in shallow bowl. Working with 1 cluster at a time and while holding by stem, dip grapes into melted chocolate; allow excess to drain back into pan. Roll grapes gently in cashews. Place grapes, stem side up, on waxed paper; repeat with remaining clusters. Refrigerate until firm. Serve within 4 hours. Garnish, if desired.

Makes about 3 dozen clusters

Triple Layer Chocolate Mints

6 ounces semisweet chocolate, chopped
6 ounces white chocolate, chopped
1 teaspoon peppermint extract
6 ounces milk chocolate, chopped

1. Line 8-inch square pan with foil, leaving 1-inch overhang on sides.

2. Place semisweet chocolate in top of double boiler over simmering water. Stir until melted. Remove from heat.

3. Spread melted chocolate onto bottom of prepared pan. Let stand until firm. (If not firm after 45 minutes, refrigerate 10 minutes.)

4. Melt white chocolate in clean double boiler; stir in peppermint extract. Spread over semisweet chocolate layer. Shake pan to spread evenly. Let stand 45 minutes or until set.

5. Melt milk chocolate in clean double boiler. Spread over white chocolate layer. Shake pan to spread evenly. Let stand 45 minutes or until set.

6. Cut mints into 16 (2-inch) squares. Remove from pan by lifting mints and foil with foil handles. Place squares on cutting board.

7. Cut each square diagonally into 2 triangles. Cut in half again to make 64 small triangles. Store in airtight container in refrigerator.

Makes 64 mints

Sinfully Simple Chocolate Cake

1 package (18¼ ounces) chocolate cake mix plus ingredients to prepare mix
1 cup whipping cream, chilled
⅓ cup chocolate syrup
Fresh fruit for garnish (optional)

1. Prepare cake mix according to package directions for two 8- or 9-inch layers. Cool layers completely.

2. Beat whipping cream with electric mixer at high speed until it begins to thicken. Gradually add chocolate syrup; continue beating until soft peaks form.

3. To assemble, place one cake layer on serving plate; spread half of whipped cream mixture over top. Set second cake layer on top; spread remaining whipped cream mixture over top. Garnish, if desired. Store in refrigerator. *Makes 12 servings*

Apple-Gingerbread Mini Cakes

1 large Cortland or Jonathan apple, cored and quartered
1 package (14½ ounces) gingerbread cake and cookie mix
1 cup water
1 egg
Powdered sugar

MICROWAVE DIRECTIONS

1. Lightly grease 10 (6- to 7-ounce) custard cups; set aside. Grate apple in food processor or with hand-held grater. Combine grated apple, cake mix, water and egg in medium bowl; stir until well blended. Spoon about ⅓ cup mix into each custard cup, filling cups half full.

2. Arrange 5 cups in microwave. Microwave at HIGH 2 minutes. Rotate cups half turn. Microwave 1 minute more or until cakes are springy when touched and look slightly moist on top. Cool on wire rack. Repeat with remaining cakes.

3. To unmold cakes, run a small knife around edge of custard cups to loosen cakes while still warm. Invert on cutting board and tap lightly until cake drops out. Place on plates. When cool enough, dust with powdered sugar, if desired. Serve warm or at room temperature.

Makes 10 cakes

Serving Suggestion: Serve with vanilla ice cream, whipped cream or crème anglaise.

Prep and Cook Time: 20 minutes

Coconut Macaroons

**1 (14-ounce) can EAGLE® BRAND Sweetened Condensed Milk
(NOT evaporated milk)**
2 teaspoons vanilla extract
1 to 1½ teaspoons almond extract
2 (7-ounce) packages flaked coconut (5⅓ cups)

1. Preheat oven to 325°F. Line baking sheets with foil; grease and flour foil. Set aside.

2. In large bowl, combine Eagle Brand, vanilla and almond extract. Stir in coconut. Drop by rounded teaspoonfuls onto prepared sheets; with spoon, slightly flatten each mound.

3. Bake 15 to 17 minutes or until golden. Remove from baking sheets; cool on wire racks. Store loosely covered at room temperature.

Makes about 4 dozen cookies

Prep Time: 10 minutes
Bake Time: 15 to 17 minutes

Fudgy Milk Chocolate Fondue

1 (16-ounce) can chocolate-flavored syrup
1 (14-ounce) can EAGLE® BRAND Sweetened Condensed Milk
    (NOT evaporated milk)
   Dash salt
1½ teaspoons vanilla extract
   Assorted dippers: cookies, cake, pound cake cubes, angel food
      cake cubes, banana chunks, apple slices, strawberries, pear
      slices, kiwifruit slices and/or marshmallows

1. In heavy saucepan over medium heat, combine syrup, Eagle Brand and salt. Cook and stir 12 to 15 minutes or until slightly thickened.

2. Remove from heat; stir in vanilla. Serve warm with assorted dippers. Store covered in refrigerator.   *Makes about 3 cups*

Microwave Directions: In 1-quart glass measure, combine syrup, Eagle Brand and salt. Cook at HIGH (100% power) 3½ to 4 minutes, stirring after 2 minutes. Stir in vanilla.

Tip: Can be served warm or cold over ice cream. Can be made several weeks ahead. Store tightly covered in refrigerator.

Prep Time: 12 to 15 minutes

Fudgy Milk Chocolate Fondue

Speedy Pineapple-Lime Sorbet

1 ripe pineapple, cut into cubes (about 4 cups)
⅓ cup frozen limeade concentrate, thawed
1 to 2 tablespoons fresh lime juice
1 teaspoon grated lime peel

1. Arrange pineapple in single layer on large sheet pan; freeze at least 1 hour or until very firm. Use metal spatula to transfer pineapple to resealable plastic freezer food storage bags; freeze up to 1 month.

2. Combine pineapple, limeade, lime juice and lime peel in food processor; process until smooth and fluffy. If pineapple doesn't become smooth and fluffy, let stand 30 minutes to soften slightly; then repeat processing. Serve immediately. Garnish as desired.

Makes 8 (½-cup) servings

quick tip

This sorbet is best if served immediately, but may be made ahead, stored in the freezer and softened several minutes before serving.

Chocolate Baskets with Berries

4 to 6 ounces semisweet or bittersweet chocolate, chopped
1 cup fresh blueberries, raspberries or sliced strawberries
2 tablespoons Grand Marnier, Chambord, Cointreau or sugar
1 cup frozen raspberry yogurt or sorbet

1. Invert two 6-ounce custard cups onto baking sheet. Cover each cup with piece of foil, smoothing surface to make sure foil stays in place. Coat foil with nonstick cooking spray.

2. Melt chocolate in small heavy saucepan over low heat. Remove from heat; let stand 10 minutes. Spoon into pastry bag fitted with small writing tip.

3. Slowly drizzle chocolate over each cup. (If chocolate drizzles too fast, let cool. If it becomes too firm, remove from bag and reheat.) Refrigerate 10 minutes. Repeat procedure; refrigerate 1 hour. Carefully remove custard cups and foil from baskets. Store in airtight container in refrigerator until ready to serve.

4. Combine fruit and liqueur in small bowl. Cover and refrigerate until ready to serve.

5. To complete recipe, spoon frozen yogurt into chocolate baskets on serving plates. Spoon fruit mixture evenly over yogurt and around chocolate baskets. Garnish as desired. *Makes 2 servings*

Make-Ahead Time: up to 1 day before serving
Final Prep and Cook Time: 5 minutes

Thumbprints

1 package (20 ounces) refrigerated sugar or chocolate cookie dough
All-purpose flour (optional)
¾ cup plus 1 tablespoon fruit preserves, any flavor

1. Grease cookie sheets. Remove dough from wrapper according to package directions. Sprinkle with flour to minimize sticking, if necessary.

2. Cut dough into 26 (1-inch) slices. Roll slices into balls, sprinkling with additional flour, if necessary. Place balls 2 inches apart on prepared cookie sheets. Press deep indentation in center of each ball with thumb. Freeze dough 20 minutes.

3. Preheat oven to 350°F. Bake cookies 12 to 13 minutes or until edges are light golden brown (cookies will have started to puff up and lose their shape). Quickly press down indentation using tip of teaspoon.

4. Return to oven 2 to 3 minutes or until cookies are golden brown and set. Cool cookies completely on cookie sheets. Fill each indentation with about 1½ teaspoons preserves.

Makes 26 cookies

Tip: These cookies are just as delicious filled with peanut butter or melted semisweet chocolate chips.

Thumbprints

Chocolate Mint Ravioli Cookies

1 package (15 ounces) refrigerated pie crusts
1 bar (7 ounces) cookies 'n' mint chocolate candy
1 egg
1 tablespoon water
  Powdered sugar

1. Preheat oven to 400°F. Unfold 1 pie crust on lightly floured surface. Roll into 13-inch circle. Using 2½-inch cutters, cut pastry into 24 circles, rerolling scraps if necessary. Repeat with remaining pie crust.

2. Separate candy bar into pieces marked on bar. Cut each chocolate piece in half. Beat egg and water together in small bowl with fork. Brush half of pastry circles lightly with egg mixture. Place 1 piece of chocolate in center of each remaining circle (there will be some candy bar left over). Top with remaining pastry circles brushed with egg mixture. Seal edges with tines of fork.

3. Place on *ungreased* baking sheets. Brush with egg mixture.

4. Bake 8 to 10 minutes or until golden brown. Remove from cookie sheets; cool completely on wire racks. Dust with powdered sugar.

Makes 2 dozen cookies

Tip: Mix it up! Substitute your favorite candy bar for the cookies 'n' mint chocolate candy for a completely different taste.

Prep and Cook Time: 30 minutes

Dashing Desserts

Spun Sugar Berries
with Yogurt Crème

2 cups fresh raspberries*
1 container (8 ounces) lemon-flavored yogurt
1 cup thawed frozen nondairy whipped topping
3 tablespoons sugar

*You may substitute your favorite fresh berries for the fresh raspberries.

1. Arrange berries in 4 glass dessert dishes.

2. Combine yogurt and whipped topping in medium bowl. (If not using immediately, cover and refrigerate.) Top berries with yogurt mixture.

3. To prepare spun sugar, pour sugar into heavy medium saucepan. Cook over medium-high heat until sugar melts, shaking pan occasionally. *Do not stir.* As sugar begins to melt, reduce heat to low and cook about 10 minutes or until sugar is completely melted and has turned light golden brown.

4. Remove from heat; let stand for 1 minute. Coat metal fork with sugar mixture. Drizzle sugar over berries with circular or back and forth motion. Ropes of spun sugar will harden quickly. Garnish as desired. Serve immediately.   *Makes 4 servings*

Banana Cream Parfaits

1 package (4 serving size) vanilla pudding and pie filling mix
2 cups milk
1 cup coarsely crushed sugar-free cookies
2 large ripe bananas, peeled and sliced
   Mint sprigs (optional)

1. Prepare pudding according to package directions using milk; cool 10 minutes, stirring occasionally.

2. In parfait or wine glasses, layer 2 tablespoons cookie crumbs, ¼ cup banana slices and ¼ cup pudding. Repeat layering. Cover; chill at least 1 hour or up to 6 hours before serving. Garnish with mint sprigs, if desired.　　　　　　　　　　　　　　　*Makes 4 servings*

Variation: Chocolate pudding and pie filling mix may be substituted for vanilla pudding.

Prep Time: 20 minutes
Cook Time: 5 minutes
Chill Time: at least 1 hour

Toffee Creme Sandwich Cookies

1 jar (7 ounces) marshmallow creme
¼ cup toffee baking pieces
48 (2-inch) sugar or fudge-striped shortbread cookies
Red and green sprinkles

1. Combine marshmallow creme and toffee pieces in medium bowl until well blended. (Mixture will be stiff.)

2. Spread 1 teaspoon marshmallow mixture on bottom of 1 cookie; top with another cookie. Roll side of sandwich cookie in sprinkles. Repeat with remaining marshmallow creme mixture, cookies and sprinkles. *Makes 2 dozen cookies*

Prep Time: 20 minutes

quick tip

Choose different colors of sprinkles to represent your favorite sports team or even just your favorite colors.

Chocolate Macadamia Chippers

1 package (18 ounces) refrigerated chocolate chip cookie dough
3 tablespoons unsweetened cocoa powder
½ cup coarsely chopped macadamia nuts

1. Preheat oven to 375°F. Remove dough from wrapper according to package directions.

2. Place dough in medium bowl; let stand 15 minutes. Stir in cocoa until well blended. (Dough may be kneaded lightly, if desired.) Stir in nuts. Drop by heaping tablespoons 2 inches apart onto ungreased cookie sheets.

3. Bake 9 to 11 minutes or until almost set. Transfer to wire racks to cool completely.   *Makes 2 dozen cookies*

Chocolate Macadamia Chippers

Walnut Meringues

   3 egg whites
   Pinch salt
¾ cup sugar
⅓ cup finely chopped walnuts

Preheat oven to 350°F. Line baking sheet with parchment paper. Place egg whites and salt in large bowl. Beat until soft peaks form. Gradually add sugar, beating until stiff peaks form. Gently fold in walnuts. Drop mounds about 1 inch in diameter 1 inch apart onto prepared baking sheet. Bake 20 minutes or until lightly browned and dry to the touch. Let cool completely before removing from baking sheet. Store in airtight container. *Makes 48 cookies*

Strawberry-Banana Granité

   2 ripe medium bananas, peeled and sliced (about 2 cups)
   2 cups unsweetened frozen strawberries *(do not thaw)*
¼ cup strawberry pourable fruit*
   Whole fresh strawberries (optional)
   Fresh mint leaves (optional)

3 tablespoons strawberry fruit spread combined with 1 tablespoon warm water may be substituted.

Place banana slices in plastic bag; freeze until firm. Place frozen banana slices and frozen strawberries in food processor container. Let stand 10 minutes for fruit to soften slightly. Add pourable fruit. Remove plunger from top of food processor to allow air to be incorporated. Process until smooth, scraping down sides of container frequently. Serve immediately. Garnish with fresh strawberries and mint leaves, if desired. Freeze leftovers. *Makes 5 servings*

Note: Granité may be transferred to airtight container and frozen up to 1 month. Let stand at room temperature 10 minutes to soften slightly before serving.

Buttery Peppermints

20 hard peppermint candies, unwrapped
5½ cups powdered sugar, divided
⅓ cup evaporated milk
¼ cup butter

1. Place peppermint candies and ½ cup powdered sugar in food processor; process using on/off pulsing action until consistency of powder.

2. Heat evaporated milk, butter and ½ cup powdered candy mixture in heavy large saucepan over medium-low heat until candy dissolves and mixture just begins to boil, stirring constantly. Transfer to large bowl. Set aside remaining powdered candy mixture.

3. Stir 4 cups powdered sugar into milk mixture with wooden spoon until well blended. Stir in additional powdered sugar, ¼ cup at a time, until consistency of dough. Place on surface lightly dusted with powdered sugar.

4. Knead dough until smooth. Divide dough into 4 equal portions.

5. Roll each portion into 20-inch-long roll. Cut each roll into ¾-inch pieces. Roll in reserved powdered candy mixture to coat.

6. For soft mints, store in airtight container at room temperature. For dry mints, keep uncovered several hours before storing in airtight container.   *Makes about 8 dozen mints*

Dashing Desserts

Luscious Chocolate Covered Strawberries

3 squares (1 ounce each) semi-sweet chocolate
2 tablespoons I CAN'T BELIEVE IT'S NOT BUTTER!® Spread
1 tablespoon coffee liqueur (optional)
6 to 8 large strawberries with stems

In small microwave-safe bowl, microwave chocolate and I Can't Believe It's Not Butter! Spread at HIGH (Full Power) 1 minute or until chocolate is melted; stir until smooth. Stir in liqueur, if desired. Dip strawberries in chocolate mixture, then refrigerate on waxed paper-lined baking sheet until chocolate is set, at least 1 hour.

Makes 6 to 8 strawberries

Surprise Cookies

1 package (18 ounces) refrigerated sugar cookie dough
All-purpose flour (optional)
Any combination of walnut halves, whole almonds, chocolate-covered raisins or caramel candy squares for filling
Assorted colored sugars

1. Grease cookie sheets. Remove dough from wrapper according to package directions. Divide dough into 4 equal sections. Reserve 1 section; cover and refrigerate remaining 3 sections.

2. Roll reserved dough to ¼-inch thickness. Sprinkle with flour to minimize sticking, if necessary. Cut out 3-inch square cookie with sharp knife. Transfer cookie to prepared cookie sheet.

3. Place desired "surprise" filling in center of cookie. (If using caramel candy square, place so that caramel forms diamond shape within square.)

4. Bring up 4 corners of dough towards center; pinch gently to seal. Repeat steps with remaining dough and fillings, placing cookies about 2 inches apart on prepared cookie sheets. Sprinkle with colored sugar, if desired. Freeze cookies 20 minutes. Preheat oven to 350°F.

5. Bake 9 to 11 minutes or until edges are lightly browned. Remove to wire racks; cool completely. *Makes about 14 cookies*

Tip: Make extra batches of these simple cookies and store in freezer in heavy-duty freezer bags. Take out a few at a time for kids' after-school treats.

Dashing Desserts

The publisher would like to thank the companies and organizations listed below for the use of their recipes and photographs in this publication.

BelGioioso Cheese, Inc.

Birds Eye Foods

Crisco is a registered trademark
of The J.M. Smucker Company

Del Monte Corporation

EAGLE BRAND®

Florida Department of Agriculture and Consumer Services,
Bureau of Seafood and Aquaculture

The Hidden Valley® Food Products Company

Holland House® is a registered trademark of Mott's, LLP

Hormel Foods, LLC

National Fisheries Institute

National Pork Board

Perdue Farms Incorporated

Reckitt Benckiser Inc.

Riviana Foods Inc.

Tyson Foods, Inc.

Unilever

USA Rice Federation™

125

Index

METRIC CONVERSION CHART

VOLUME MEASUREMENTS (dry)

1/8 teaspoon = 0.5 mL
1/4 teaspoon = 1 mL
1/2 teaspoon = 2 mL
3/4 teaspoon = 4 mL
1 teaspoon = 5 mL
1 tablespoon = 15 mL
2 tablespoons = 30 mL
1/4 cup = 60 mL
1/3 cup = 75 mL
1/2 cup = 125 mL
2/3 cup = 150 mL
3/4 cup = 175 mL
1 cup = 250 mL
2 cups = 1 pint = 500 mL
3 cups = 750 mL
4 cups = 1 quart = 1 L

VOLUME MEASUREMENTS (fluid)

1 fluid ounce (2 tablespoons) = 30 mL
4 fluid ounces (1/2 cup) = 125 mL
8 fluid ounces (1 cup) = 250 mL
12 fluid ounces (1 1/2 cups) = 375 mL
16 fluid ounces (2 cups) = 500 mL

WEIGHTS (mass)

1/2 ounce = 15 g
1 ounce = 30 g
3 ounces = 90 g
4 ounces = 120 g
8 ounces = 225 g
10 ounces = 285 g
12 ounces = 360 g
16 ounces = 1 pound = 450 g

DIMENSIONS

1/16 inch = 2 mm
1/8 inch = 3 mm
1/4 inch = 6 mm
1/2 inch = 1.5 cm
3/4 inch = 2 cm
1 inch = 2.5 cm

OVEN TEMPERATURES

250°F = 120°C
275°F = 140°C
300°F = 150°C
325°F = 160°C
350°F = 180°C
375°F = 190°C
400°F = 200°C
425°F = 220°C
450°F = 230°C

BAKING PAN SIZES

Utensil	Size in Inches/Quarts	Metric Volume	Size in Centimeters
Baking or Cake Pan (square or rectangular)	8×8×2	2 L	20×20×5
	9×9×2	2.5 L	23×23×5
	12×8×2	3 L	30×20×5
	13×9×2	3.5 L	33×23×5
Loaf Pan	8×4×3	1.5 L	20×10×7
	9×5×3	2 L	23×13×7
Round Layer Cake Pan	8×1½	1.2 L	20×4
	9×1½	1.5 L	23×4
Pie Plate	8×1¼	750 mL	20×3
	9×1¼	1 L	23×3
Baking Dish or Casserole	1 quart	1 L	—
	1½ quart	1.5 L	—
	2 quart	2 L	—